AF440531

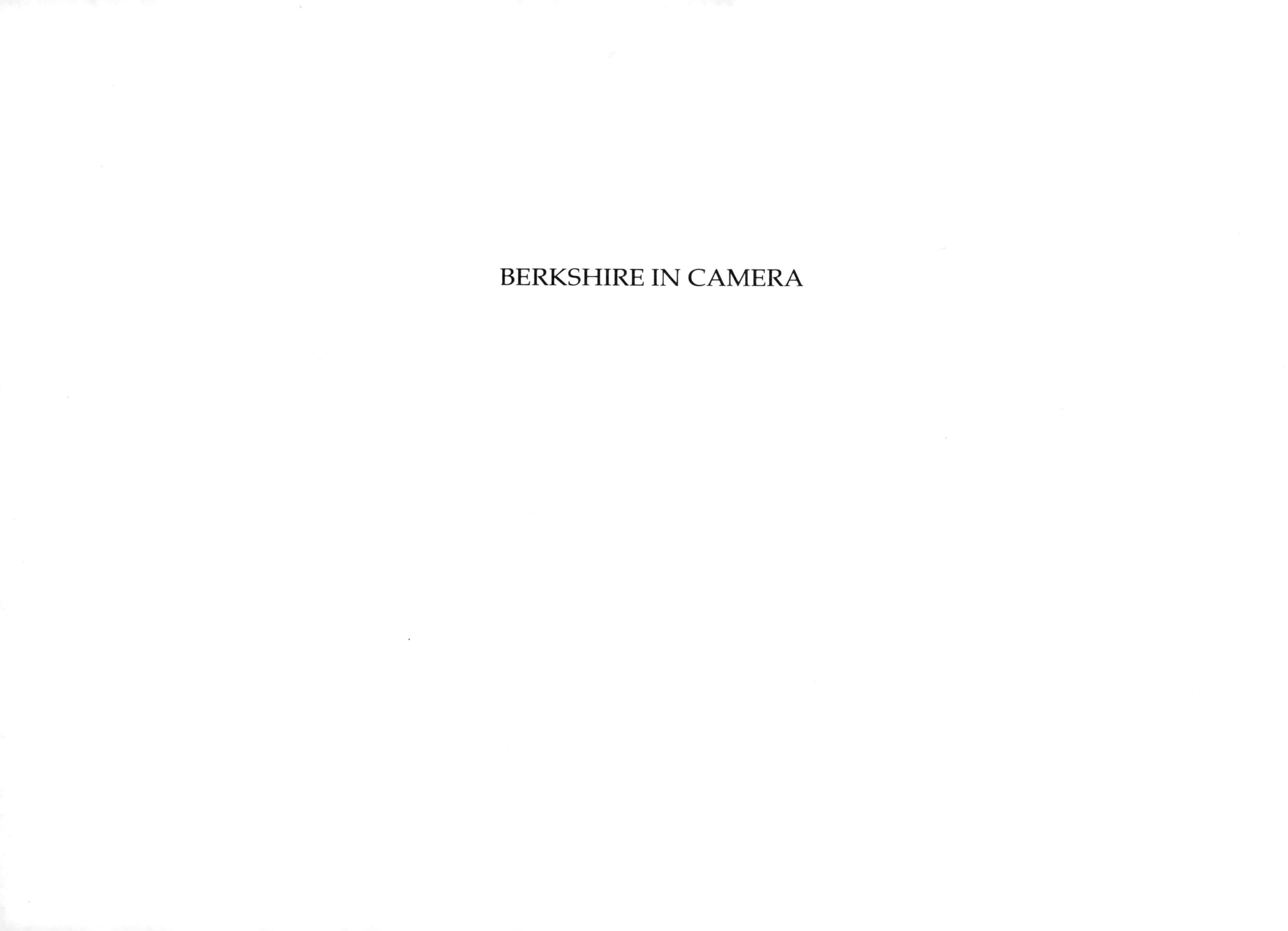

BERKSHIRE IN CAMERA

SUSAN READ

BERKSHIRE IN CAMERA

Berkshire and the Vale of the White Horse 1845-1920

Published jointly by
Countryside Books, and Reading Museum and Art Gallery

First Published 1981
© Reading Museum and Art Gallery 1981
All rights reserved. No reproduction
permitted without the
prior permission of the publishers:
Countryside Books
3 Catherine Road
Newbury, Berkshire

ISBN 0 905392 10 8

The cover photograph of East Ilsley was taken
by Henry Taunt in about 1895

Designed by Mon Mohan & Alison Lees
Printed in England by
Lonsdale Universal Printing Ltd., Bath

Contents

Introduction   7

Berkshire Towns 17

Berkshire Villages 27

People at Work 39

People at Play 50

People at Rest 56

The Berkshire Home: Cottage, Farm and Mansion 59

The Berkshire Home: Interiors 64

The Berkshire Home: Gardens 65

River and Canal 68

Road 77

Rail 83

Celebrations 88

Acknowledgements 95

Index 96

Introduction

It is strange to think what our knowledge of the nineteenth and early twentieth centuries would have been without the watchful eye of the camera. We accept the history of past centuries from remaining ruins, standing buildings and written records – but how much more closely can we relate to the Victorian and Edwardian eras through the undeniable reality of the people and places captured in their photographs.

In the nineteenth century Berkshire, unlike other parts of Britain, was not confronted by the arrival of industrial chimneys on every skyline. But indirectly the effects of industrial development were far reaching. Pressures on the agricultural labourer had been mounting over the centuries with the desire for more intensive farming and the enclosure of previously held common land. Better prospects and higher wages lured many away from the traditional country background to merge into the new and rapidly growing town communities.

One of the new manufacturing industries was the famous firm of Huntley and Palmers, the Biscuit Makers of Reading, who developed their trade to cover a national and even international market. In 1864 the firm claimed that their products travelled as far afield as 'Greenland to Cochin China, Nova Zembla to New Zealand'. The resulting success and increase in prosperity enabled them to expand a staff of 143 in 1851 to 5,057 in 1900. These employees were able to benefit directly from the Victorian paternal attitude of the employer for his staff. In the case of Huntley and Palmers this concern for their welfare resulted in the introduction of sickness benefits, sports clubs, library facilities and even schooling for the youngest boys employed.

Unfortunately, those who remained in the country to work on the land found themselves faced with a rather more bleak outlook. The importing of many foods from abroad decreased the amount of produce needed from the English farmer. Hence the wages which he could afford to pay did not compare with those offered by a town employer. In the past the cottager had maintained his family through self-sufficiency, growing food and keeping a few animals on his own land and that common to the manor. Being debarred from this land by the Enclosure Acts was a severe blow. More and more he found himself forced to rely on being a wage-earner to make sure that he had sufficient money for the rent of his cottage and his ever increasing dependence on shop-bought items. It is hardly surprising that the younger generation sought early employment in service in country houses as well as in towns. The temptation to emigrate to other parts of the world, offering more challenging and potentially prosperous horizons, such as Australia and South Africa, was very real.

However, within both town and country there were other large and important social groups. The comfortably off middle range farmers did not suffer with the agricultural labourers but greatly benefited from the advances in agricultural practices. The towns, on the other hand, were not a source of prosperity for all their inhabitants. The already well established communities of urban poor grew in numbers since insufficient work, housing and other facilities were available for the rapidly increasing population. And at this point it should be made clear that the majority of the early photographers wanted picturesque views to sell to the wealthier classes. With the exception of a few photographers including Dr. Barnardo and the American Jacob Riis who paid special attention to social hardship, the camera was not yet focused on the scenes of real squalor in the lives of the urban and rural poor which are depicted, for instance, in the Punch cartoons of the period.

Centrally placed in southern England, Berkshire was able to take full advantage of the improvements in communications which developed in the nineteenth century. Reading and Newbury had always benefited from their position on major trading routes. However the coming of the railway to the county in the 1840s introduced a new era. Such a speedy and convenient way of transporting goods and people could not have been previously imagined. From east to west, Brunel's iron artery of the Great Western Railway was constructed. This was in due course supplemented by many smaller lines such as the Lambourn Valley Line, all of which were vital links in the overall network of the new and revolutionary means of communication.

Improvements to the roads were striking after the arrival of the motor car at the turn of the century. Faced by such strong competition from rail and road, the rivers and canals of Berkshire strove to maintain their important function, but by the end of the century waterborne traffic was becoming less involved with transporting commercial goods and more with facilities for pleasure craft. Travelling for pleasure was suddenly a reality for ordinary people as more money and time became available for this pursuit. The improved means of transport allowed a greater opportunity to travel on old and new routeways throughout the county and previously unknown areas became accessible to the traveller on business and pleasure alike.

A way of life that had lasted for centuries was coming to an end. The people must have been aware of how fundamentally life was changing, but it was the camera that vividly and faithfully recorded the twilight hours of one era, and the bursting rays of a new dawning.

Berkshire has a surprisingly close connection with the very earliest days of photography. It was the acknowledged 'Father of Photography' in Britain, William Henry Fox Talbot, who chose to set up his first photographic establishment in Reading. This energetic and extremely gifted country gentleman found the town to be an ideal situation between London and his family seat at Lacock Abbey in Wiltshire. A small house in Baker Street, just outside the centre of the town, was selected to house both his equipment and his assistant Nicolaas Henneman. (See 1.) It was here from 1843 to 1846 that further photographic experiments were pursued following the success of his invention of the Calotype or Talbotype in

1   Fox Talbot's photographic Establishment in Baker Street, Reading 1843 – 1846. Here photographic work is in process at the back of the premises.

1839. This process had taken the world by storm as it was the first to produce a negative from which a print could be made. However, this was a paper negative and was to be superseded in the future first by the wet plate method invented in 1857 and then by the dry plate or gelatin emulsion process which was available on the open market in 1873.

The most important result of Fox Talbot's short stay in Reading was the production of the first book in the world illustrated with photographs. 'The Pencil of Nature' has been compared in uniqueness to the Gutenberg Bible and not more than 24 complete copies are known to exist. The

2   St George's Chapel Windsor
     A calotype taken by Fox Talbot c. 1846

beautiful photographs contained in it are a fitting memorial to the pioneer Fox Talbot and also to the introduction and establishment of photography. There are a number of existing photographs of Berkshire taken by Fox Talbot, including that of St George's Chapel, Windsor. (See 2.)

Who were the photographers in Berkshire who followed in the footsteps of Fox Talbot? The 1850s saw the gradual establishment of the commercial photographer. The early 'photographic artists', so classified in the local directories, started up in competition with the small studio portrait artists. Yet unlike the medium of the traditional artist, this new art form which they were pursuing was continuously developing faster and cheaper production methods. In the Kelly's Berkshire Directory for 1864 there were fourteen photographic artists scattered through the main towns; by 1877 there were twenty-three.

Photography, in particular the portrait, developed from the 'Daguerreotype' – introduced in 1839 by the Frenchman Louis Daguerre. (See 3.) The surface of the Daguerreotype has a mirror like appearance as the image is on a highly polished copper plate coated with silver. The exposure time required was originally 15 to 20 minutes and, though suitable for taking a building or still life, the portrait posed much greater problems. Any movement would be disastrous and the studio photographer had to resort to a head clamp for his sitters. Fortunately, it was only a short while before the exposure times were reduced although even then these were often uncomfortably long in comparison with those possible in modern photography.

This was followed in 1851 by the 'Ambrotype', a positive photograph on a glass plate, which in its turn was challenged within two years by the cheaper and quicker method using an enamelled metal plate – the 'Ferrotype' or 'Tintype'. All of these were small in size and were fitted into metal frames or moulded leather cases in the form of a book with a clasp. A drawback to these processes was that only a single image could be produced without a negative. This was not the case with the other well-known type of small portrait photograph – the 'carte-de-visite'. (See 4 & 5.) Introduced in the 1850s the photograph usually measured 3½" × 2½" and was mounted on a card which frequently acted as an elaborate form of advertisement for the photographer. (See 6 & 7.) The great asset of this method of production was that exact copy photographs could be printed from the negative. Other photographs of this type included the larger cabinet photograph. (See 8.) Speed in production may have reduced quality in some instances but the quantity of output from this new breed of while-you-wait photographers was undeniable. For the first time a form of natural portrait was brought within the financial means of a far wider section of the public. The numerous treasured family albums which have survived, of cartes-de-visite in particular, illustrate the pleasure of this as a collecting hobby.

The other contribution made by the early commercial photographers was that of views and scenes of nearby towns, villages, and countryside. This was a far from easy task in the early days before the invention of the dry plate method due to the amount of equipment required to be transported in addition to the camera. Nevertheless for the 'outdoor' photographer the production of photographs and later postcards was to prove not only very popular but financially extremely worthwhile. The public were led into

3 A daguerreotype of George Loveday (1808-1883) – the Reading bookseller and library owner c. 1848

the enjoyment of owning a photograph of their familiar surroundings, whether a beautiful view of a well-loved stretch of river, the bustle of a familiar town street, or possibly a special occasion or national celebration. These photographs could be collected in albums to give pleasure

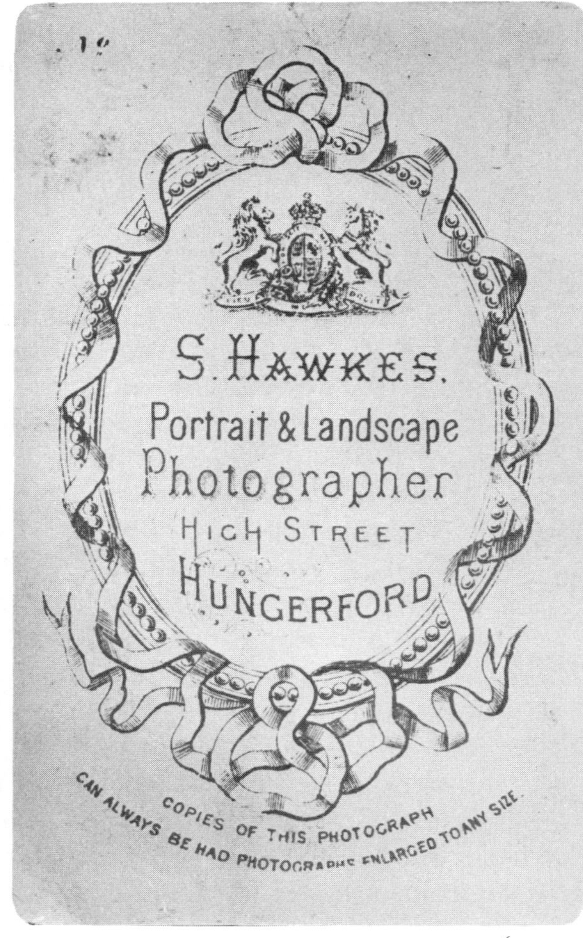

4   Carte-de-Visite. Taken by the Reading photographer
     W S Wyles of 101-103 Kings Road 1880 – 1908. c. 1890

5   Carte-de-Visite. Taken by the Reading photographer
     W S Wyles of 101-103 Kings Road 1880 – 1908. c. 1900

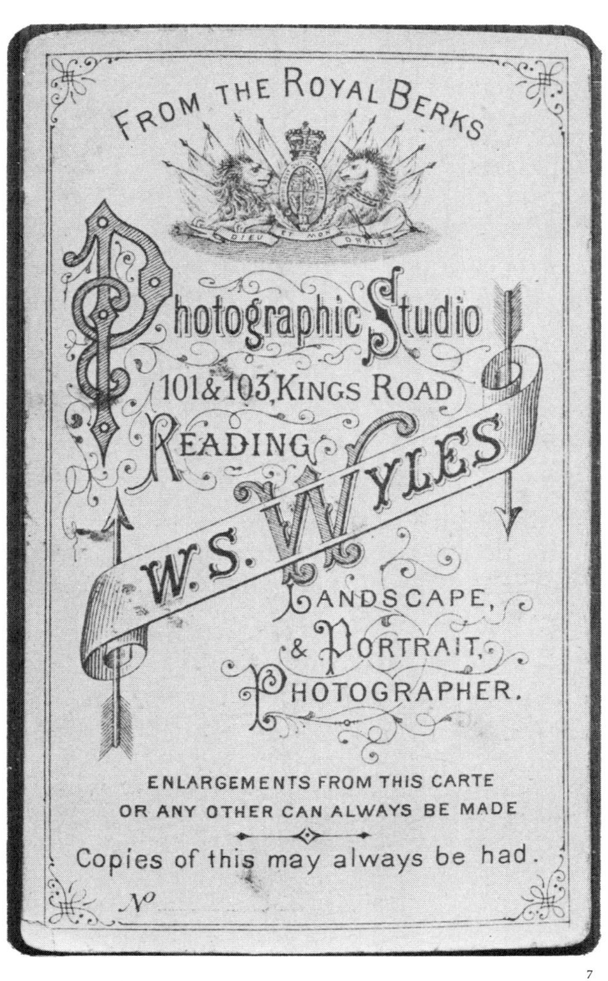

6&7 The backs of two cartes-de-visite advertising
photographers from Hungerford and Reading c. 1895

8   A cabinet portrait of a grandmother and grandaughter
from a family in Shinfield c. 1890

on long winter evenings, or framed and placed on permanent view on the parlour wall. The introduction of the post card in the 1880s opened up a further field for collecting as well as a new and rapidly popular vogue for sending cards to friends and relatives. By the turn of the century stationers' shops stacked from floor to ceiling with views and greetings cards were a familiar sight in the large towns.

Photography in the Victorian period was not only a professional and commercial pursuit. The enthusiastic amateur was soon on the scene and, as the cost of equipment and materials became cheaper, the art of photography fell within the reach of many more people. In an era when hobbies were increasingly popular, photography as a hobby was taken up by both men and women. Here was scope to combine practical knowledge of the camera with the creativity of the artist. Looking at such photographs today one can see that the results varied enormously with so many factors involved. These included the standard of equipment, the lighting and weather conditions and, of course, the steady hand and knowing eye of the photographer. However, one does discover some extremely good and, more important, unique views and subjects taken by amateur photographers which greatly enhance our knowledge and understanding of the times in which they were taken.

At this point I should like to introduce a particular commercial photographer Henry Taunt, to whom as a county we can be very grateful and whose photographs I have used widely in this book. Henry W. Taunt was born in Oxford in 1842 with a partly Berkshire background as his mother came from West Ilsley. He made his way into photography as an assistant in one of the photographic studios in Oxford. His early days of photography were centred on his own particular love – the Thames. This culminated in a much acclaimed topographical publication 'A New Map of the River Thames' in 1872. By branching out on his own he was able to establish a shop in Oxford and a small printing works on the outskirts of the city. A catalogue of 1874 offered copy photographs from over 3,000 negatives taken by Taunt and his assistants. These covered the counties of Oxfordshire, Berkshire, and Buckinghamshire with additional views of some of the adjacent counties. Subjects were numerous to cover many aspects of scenery and life, be it of countryside or town, and he was always ready 'on request' to photograph 'Gentlemen's Seats, Churches, Interiors, Groups, etc.' His photographs were artistic works in their own right and were recognised for their excellence of quality. 'Amongst them are some which for softness and clearness of detail, as well as effective reproduction of light and shade, rival in beauty the work of the most skilled draughtsman.' The Field. 16 December 1871.

Many of his photographs were specifically of buildings. As official photographer to the Oxford Architectural and Historical Society, he was only too aware of the necessity to record these. In fact, whether building, landscape, or custom, he was conscious of the many changes which were already taking effect before his death in 1922.

The purpose of this book is to create a picture of Berkshire as seen through the lens of the early photographers. I have attempted to cover a wide range of places and people throughout the Old and New County of Berkshire from the earliest days of photography through the changing eras up to 1920. I am very much aware that a number of villages and views are not represented and for this I would like to offer my apologies. But I am encouraged by the thought that the book may lead to new discoveries – already a number of previously unknown photographs have come to light during my search for pictures. The photographs come from a variety of sources. Some are from large public collections such as the National Buildings Record in London, the Museum of English Rural Life in Reading, and the County Libraries of Berkshire and Oxfordshire. The Berkshire Archaeological Society has its own large collection of glass negatives housed at Reading Museum. Other equally important photographs have been provided by private individuals.

Dating early photographs can be a problem, often one has to rely on the changing fashions in clothing worn by the people in the photographs, or a dateable new method of transport. Where the name of the shopkeeper or other commercial firm is visible it is possible to trace when they were in business through the contemporary local directories which are held by main libraries and the County Record Office. One is always hoping to build up additional information and I should be very pleased to receive any

further details connected with the photographs here to add to our Museum records.

The survival of photographs, and in particular of negatives, has been fortuitous, considering the hazards that may befall them – fire, flood, fading and breakage are but a few. Perhaps the saddest is when the person or scene in the photograph becomes detached from its history and no living memory can recall nor recognise it. Many individuals and local groups are doing very good work on recording photographs in their own areas. If photographs can be borrowed from their owners and copied, the likelihood of their survival into the future will be made more secure. For it is this link with the past that can be our gift to the future.

'All photographs have some limited historical value; those taken today will many of them be much wanted in fifty years time'.

H W TAUNT 1918

REPAIRS IN ALL BRANCHES

Berkshire Towns

THE arrival of photography coincided with a period in which the towns of Berkshire began to alter their traditional role as centres for the surrounding agricultural communities. The invention and continuous improvement of machinery encouraged the development of manufacturing industries in the towns. Improved communications and in particular the arrival of the railways in the 1840s opened up new markets for an increasing range of products. Two of the major employers in Reading at the turn of the century, Sutton Seeds and Huntley and Palmers, would not have been able to expand as they did without an efficient railway network and postal service.

Agriculture, however, still remained the largest commercial influence and consideration for most Berkshire towns in this period. The weekly markets continued to cater for the needs of the inhabitants for food and other household goods. Agricultural fairs on a much larger scale were held on specific dates during the year, and continued to be the highpoint for buying and selling cattle and sheep. The importance of the Corn Exchanges in the towns is prominently shown in photographs 12 and 18. Many of these were built in the middle of the nineteenth century. Although the early commerce and industry of the towns had centred on agricultural products, such as the woollen and brewing industries, new developments encouraged other manufacturing industries which included iron-foundries and brickworks.

From a cluster of houses and shops and other small business premises, the towns expanded noticeably in the nineteenth century, and the camera played a unique part in faithfully documenting this growth and change.

A street scene often contrasts the old, frequently dilapidated buildings with the crisp new ones, often in locally made brick. The presence of more numerous and varied types of shops highlights the benefits of the Victorian commercial enterprise. Alterations in modes of transport are immediately noticeable. The horse-drawn wagons, carts, and traps are replaced by trams and motor vehicles which inevitably set a new pace on town life. Signs of improved street maintenance catch the eye – the road surface, the pavements, and lighting. Certainly town life offered the camera a golden opportunity for its 'love of detail'. The names and signwriting on the shops, the articles for sale on display in the windows, advertisements for goods, theatres and local events and, of course, the people themselves in their rich variety of dress. Some photographs even manage to convey the feeling of old street sounds and smells!

9   Faringdon c. 1904 (opposite)
Apart from the weekly market, Faringdon had four major agricultural fairs during the year. With its central position in an important part of the country for dairy production – these became well-known events. The main area of the town was taken over for animal pens, and farm carts. In the background a large piece of modern farm machinery (an elevator for hoisting sheaves during rick building and threshing) has been set up for inspection. Shrewd business is the main feature of the day but the children certainly appear to be making the most of the occasion.

10

10   Windsor c.1865
An early photographic view of the castle and part of the town across the river from the Brocas.

11   Maidenhead c.1890 (right)
Here at the Kings Street Post Office the actual posting box is almost lost amongst the display of pipes and tobacco. Some of the names advertised are still well-known today. An interesting addition to the items for sale is the collection of walking sticks just inside the door, advertised as being "in great variety". The Post Office also displays posters for local entertainments. The bill-board at the door announces a performance of 'Hans the Boatman' at the Grand Hall, Maidenhead.

11

12   Newbury c.1890
A traditionally thriving scene in the market place on market day – Thursday. Men, women, and children wend their way from stall to stall viewing the various goods for sale. The carts, carriages, and covered wagons belong to both sellers and buyers, including the travelling carriers collecting orders for the outlying villages. The Old Waggon and Horses Inn advertises Hawkins, who was a Newbury brewer and wine and spirit merchant. The imposing building in the centre is owned by the London and County Banking Company.

13   Maidenhead c.1890
Market Street caught at a busy time of the day when the children are on the way home from school, the smallest girl in the centre carrying a writing slate under her arm. Shoe shops are already numerous with Good & Wyatt on the corner, and a few doors further down the street a large sign advertises "Symmons & Hewitt, Boot & Shoe Department". The street sign to North Town and Cookham has additional character with its drawing of a pointing hand. The majority of the little girls are wearing the white pinafores, straw hats, and buttoned boots typical of the period, whilst the boys sport knee breeches and caps.

14 Newbury c.1890 (opposite)
"There is an iron clock tower erected in the Broadway, 30 ft in height, with four illuminated dials for ornamental bracket lamps and two drinking fountains at a cost of £278.5s subscribed by the townspeople. The Russian gun was also placed in the Broadway." Kelly's Directory for 1891. The latter was probably a relic of the Crimean War.

15 Abingdon c.1899
A view taken in Ock Street. The style of decorative sign writing on the shop belonging to J Leonard is outstanding. This also gives clear details of the diversity of his trade – "Plumber, Glazier, Gas and Water Fitter, Painter, Paper Hanger, Writer, Grainer, Decorator". The well-made pavements have a band of cobble stones to strengthen the edging. At this time the streets continued to be lit by gas supplied in Abingdon by a company formed in 1834.

16 Wokingham c.1900
Looking down from Shute End towards the clock tower. As at Wantage (see 19), we find the ironmonger's business flourishing including the facilities for cycle repairs, and the Cyclists Touring Club plaque. The shops and houses show an alteration in styles and a building line common to gradual town development over the centuries. The children are obviously intrigued by the presence of the photographer.

17 Reading c.1910 (left)
Market Way Arcade. A view of the spacious shopping arcade running between Broad Street and Friar Street. The small open fronted shops offer various goods for sale, including the large Huntley and Palmers biscuit tins at the opening to the shop nearest the camera. Although well designed to allow as much natural light as possible, this was supplemented by gas lights hanging in pairs. The arcade was badly damaged in an air raid in 1943.

18 Hungerford c.1900
Looking down High Street with the clock tower and corn exchange on the left. These wide streets were typical of country towns enabling markets to be held without inconvenience to the thoroughfare.

19   Wantage c.1901 (previous page)
The Market Place here depicts a typical centre of commercial townlife with shop goods displayed not only on the pavements but even in the road. The outfitters on the far left has a marvellous selection of boots hanging outside the shop, whilst the written advertisement offers "Suits to Measure, Good Style and Fit at Lowest Cash Prices". Equally eyecatching is Mrs Dixon's Milliners small shop two doors along the street, with its windows full of straw hats. On the wall of Kent and Sons Ironmongers Shop is a plaque of the C T C – the Cyclists Touring Club. Cycling was a popular pastime and not only has this shop plenty of cycles for sale outside but also A J Belcher, the ironmonger on the left, displays a sign – "Agency for Rudge Whitworth Cycles".

20   Reading c.1910 (below left)
The family butcher's business of W & R Fletcher Ltd. dates back to the 19th century. The photographer could not have caught a more perfect pose of the staff of a butcher's shop against this extensive array of meat joints tempting the customer. The butcher in the doorway has hanging from his waist a steel for sharpening the heavy butcher's knives. The assistant on the left is holding the hooked pole ready to pull out the protecting shop awning. The young boy wearing a cap is the delivery lad who would make his rounds by bicycle.

21   Wallingford c.1911
Looking up St. Mary's Street from St. Leonard's Lane towards the centre of the town. Facing one another across the street are the two public houses the Royal Standard on the right, and the Coachmaker's Arms on the left.

22 Reading c.1900
A horse-drawn tram in the Oxford Road with Reading West railway bridge in the background. The Reading Tramway Company operated horse trams from 1879, running a route along Oxford Road, Broad Street, and King's Road to Cemetery Junction.
The tram had a staircase and a position for the driver at both ends, so that it was not necessary to turn the vehicle, only to reharness the horses. Pairs of horses usually worked in rotation with the fifth day at rest. The working life of a tram horse was unlikely to be more than four years, as it was very hard work. Not only were they pulling the weight of the trams and passengers, but the rails naturally became choked with dirt and refuse. The poor state of the horses was one of the reasons for the take over by the Corporation Tramway Company, and the last horse tram was seen in Reading in 1903.

23 Reading c.1908
An electric tram at the terminus on Caversham Road just before Caversham Bridge. The old horse drawn system of the Reading Tramways Company was taken over by Reading Corporation Tramways in 1901. There followed a programme of complete electrification using overhead cables. New routes were introduced with termini in London Road, Erleigh Road, Whitley Street, Bath Road, and Caversham Road. Reading continued to be well-known for its trams until their final closure in 1939.

Berkshire Villages

THE numerous villages throughout the Berkshire countryside were a natural and vital sign of a county with its roots deeply planted in rich agricultural soil. The traditional village scenes of the eighteenth century watercolour artists suddenly became more real through the eye of the camera, despite their being in black and white. The main street, the village lanes, the green with its cluster of cottages, the parental shadow of the church, and the solid character of the village inn are joined by newcomers – the post office, the school, and the fire station.

The atmosphere of most pictures is one of peace and calm, almost sleepy in places. Was this perhaps due to the photographer choosing a weekday visit when most people would have been busy working elsewhere? Certainly many village views lack human life. However when people are caught in the midst of their daily routine, they usually appear well aware of the photographer – sometimes curious, sometimes shy. To them the sight of a camera must have been less familiar than to townsfolk.

The villages in the photographs here present a picture of rosy arcadia: a wholesome tribute to the benefits of the good life. The reality was that village life could be just as squalid as town life with a good deal of poverty, overcrowding, and hunger, as many official reports of the period make clear. However, the camera as an instrument for social comment was still a long way off. The early interest of the photographer and those who might buy his pictures was in a rural scene which was carefree and relaxed.

24 Steventon c.1855 (opposite)
The photographer who took this scene in the very early days of the camera, was using Fox Talbot's Calotype process – as mentioned in the introduction. In common with any artist, he found the rustic charm of the barn and cart worthy of a permanent record.

25 Ruscombe c.1860
The School at Vale Cottage. The 'dame school' was a familiar sight before the introduction of compulsory education in 1870. A small weekly fee was paid by the pupils to the dame or mistress, who held the classes in her own private house. The standard of teaching naturally varied, but this is how one mistress described her work:

"I teach them to read, and to sew, and the Belief and the Commandments, and them little things."

26   North Hinksey c.1880
F.G. Brabant in his book on Berkshire (1911) describes well the event in this photograph:
> "This was the scene of Ruskin's attempt to utilise the muscle of Oxford (undergraduates) in roadmaking instead of cricket and football. But the road experimented on is just as muddy as it was before."

27   Cookham c.1890
This heavy cladding of ivy on the church tower is not a sight that we would expect to see today. However, in general many church exteriors and interiors have remained unchanged since the introduction of photography. Numerous early photographs of churches are found as this has always been a popular subject.

28

29

28 Bisham c.1890
The village street at Bisham is caught at a busy moment in the day. Beer, on a brewer's dray, is being delivered to the Bull Inn which offered 'Pale Ale Stout & Porter' from Langton's, a Maidenhead brewery. Opposite, a carrier's cart has stopped outside a typical row of 19th century chequered brick cottages.

29 Aldworth c.1890 (right)
The Lychgate to St Mary's church. The famous yew tree is just off the photograph to the left. This was described in Kelly's Directory 1891 as "an excellent yew tree measuring nine yards round the trunk and supposed to be older than the church". The young lady in the shadow of the gate is wearing a fashionable boater and style of sleeves current at this period.

30 Waltham St Lawrence c.1895 (left)
Looking up the village street from the church and pound. The few people about are enjoying a quiet summer's day, with long shadows being cast by the sun accross the road. The clarity of the tricycle has all but disappeared as the camera is unable to cope with the speed of movement.

31 Bray c.1895 (above)
The church of St Michael overlooks this peaceful village scene. Like most villages, Bray is well supplied with public houses including 'The Ringers' on the right and 'The Hind's Head' in the centre. Village roads are still not made up and one can pick out the carriage and cart wheels in the flattened bare earth. This late 19th century view contrasts the small and irregular timber framed buildings on the right with the taller, more severe and solid, later brick houses on the opposite side of the street.

32   Sonning c.1899

This view contrasts the variations in building styles characteristic of a village growing over the centuries. The chimneys in particular catch the eye. The solid external stack placed at the end of the cottage is very different in design to the decorative Victorian stacks and chimney pots on the building across the road. The two little girls add a further touch to the scene.

33   Three Mile Cross c.1900

The following passage from Miss Mitford's 'Our Village' describes the wheelright's shop and house pictured here:

'We are now at the end of the street; a cross-lane, a rope-walk shaded with limes and oaks, and a cool clear pond overhung with elms, lead us to the bottom of the hill. There is still one house round the corner, ending in a picturesque wheeler's shop. The dwelling house is more ambitious. Look at the fine flowered window blinds, the green door with the brass knocker, and the somewhat prim but very civil person, who is sending off a labouring man with sirs and curtsies enough for a prince of the blood. Those are the curate's lodgings – apartments his landlady would call them; he lives with his own family four miles off, but once or twice a week he comes to his neat little parlour to write sermons, to marry, or to bury as the case may require.'

34   Pangbourne c.1900
Here in the village street the carrier's cart belonging to J Rumble stands to the right of the photograph. This service covered the villages of 'Yattendon, Frilsham, Marlston, Hermitage, Burnt Hill, Pangbourne, Reading and Newbury' running to Reading on Wednesday and Saturday, and Newbury on Tuesday and Thursday. It offered passenger transport and acted as a 'universal shopper' collecting goods for all the villages.

35   Goosey c.1905
At this time a fairly extensive restoration on the church was carried out, including replacing the bell cot. Fortunately it was one of the churches which was sympathetically restored, for during the Victorian period many suffered the fate of being demolished and completely rebuilt.

36   East Hagbourne c.1904 (opposite)
This village scene had been well described in Kelly's Directory 1895. "N. East of the church and in the village stands a fine cross on lofty steps. There are some extremly picturesque and good examples here of timber and plaster, or tile-fronted houses, several of which, the property of Lord Wantage, have been carefully restored".
The attention paid to the cottages here and on the main Lockinge Estate by Lord Wantage provides a good example of the owner's attitude to his responsibility. Equally of interest is his source of income for this work which was from his commercial banking pursuits, unlike the majority of landowners who relied on income from agriculture.

37   East Ilsley 1906
High Street. The figures in the distance are clustered around sheep pens, showing one of the fairs in progress, hence the notice leaning against the wall of the Swan offering Rams and Lambs for sale. Commercial hotels such as the Swan and the Crown opposite were in great demand during the fairs. On the left is the shop of the family butcher and farmer Mark Wells, with his solid farm cart drawn up outside. Over the window hangs a striped blind to protect the shop and produce from heat and the dust of the road.

38   Yattendon c.1909 (above right)
An example of the traditional village shop which catered for every need. Above the doorway of the house attached to the shop is a poster advertising the British Army.
The shopkeeper at Yattendon at this time was a Mr 'Bumper' Ward who was also a gifted amateur photographer. The fate of his collection of glass negatives after his death is a familar story, for they were used as cloches in the garden.

39   Bradfield c.1910 (opposite)
A popular method of making greetings cards was to include a photograph of an attractive village scene, with some additional artistic and poetic licence! These cottages beside the Pang River provided an ideal subject.

40   Shrivenham c.1915 (opposite)
The village pump was another traditional feature of village life. In areas where not every household had a private well, this provided a very necessary general water supply. It was equally important for the traveller by horse. The family gathered here beneath the pump make a charming study for the photographer. The baby's high-wheeled pram is particularly intriguing.

WITH
LOVING
GREETINGS

The flight of years
cannot divide
Hearts that are true
Love that is tried.

GOOD
WISHES
GALORE.

41   Stanford-in-the-Vale c.1915 (opposite)
A village scene taken on the upper green. The young people of the village symbolize the changing generations, in contrast with the stability of the old buildings behind. The farmhouse on the right has special stones above the gable windows marked with the date of its construction, 1670. These also bear the initials IY and HY, probably members of the Yates family who built the house.

42   Charney Bassett c.1915
The Chequers Inn is attached behind, on the left to yet another public house, the Horn. The smithy on the right of the photograph is well sited next door to the two pubs. At this time a William Kerridge ran both the the Chequers Inn and the smithy.

43   Hinton Waldrist 1915
The village shop and post office at this time was owned by Clare
Richards. The children seem to be intrigued by the camera and have
stopped in their play to pose. Although slightly stiff they should be
congratulated for not moving. They are wearing the traditional white
pinafores and knee breeches, and a marvellous array of hats and caps.

44   Childrey c.1915 (right)
R. Heading, Butcher and Grocer. The shop and cottage clearly show the
traditional chequered and patterned Berkshire brickwork. No longer do
these open directly onto the village street but allowance is made for a
small area of neatly-kept front garden.

People at Work

Photographing people at work has always offered interest and a challenge to the photographer. The countryside and the village provided plenty of suitable subjects in the Victorian period, whether haymaking in the fields, or the individual craftsman at his work. As the century drew to a close these sights became more rare, and their continuing fascination to the photographer may have been due partly to a feeling of nostalgia for a passing era. Scenes of agricultural labouring begin to show signs of mechanization, particularly after the arrival of the steam traction engines. In the villages the various craftsmen on whom the community had depended faced a reduction in numbers, often leaving only the blacksmith coping with minor repairs of machinery and eventually cars. The turning years brought new occupations to the towns rather than the villages. Trade and industry introduced more shopkeepers and their assistants, and greatly increased the number of factory workers. The skills of the photographer and the early camera were put to the test with moving figures and working machinery, especially with interior views where natural light was lacking.

45

45   Wittenham 1885 (right)
    Caught in action during the rebuilding of Day's Lock weir. Fortunately the men appear to have frozen in their movement for the sake of the photograph. This and other rebuilding along the Thames in the latter part of the 19th century greatly increased the safety for both commercial and pleasure craft. The steam engine on the right is a portable model, but would have required horses to bring it to the site.

46   Reading c.1890 (following page)
    In the yard of Simonds Brewery. On the left the large brewer's drays are loaded and the drivers presumably are awaiting the word to proceed on the day's deliveries. In front are two of the smaller, single horse, brewer's floats. Simonds Brewery house was designed in the late 18th century and demolished in 1900.

46

47

48

47 Maidenhead c.1890 (above)
Haymaking here is on a very different scale to that on the Wantage Estate at Lockinge (52). Every member of the family, regardless of age, has an important part to play. In the background is Maidenhead Goods Station.

48 Maidenhead c.1890 (below left)
James Hews, Ironmonger 95, High Street. The photographer has made a conscious effort to capture the working atmosphere of the building and the men. However, perhaps the most outstanding feature of the photograph is the expression and underlying character caught in the individual faces.

49 Newbury c.1895 (opposite)
The large porch is an unusual addition to this type of barn, and appears to have been made from reused early timbers. The farm workers are wearing the traditional country smocks. The smaller of the two carts is being pulled by a donkey. To the left of the barn is the old Fire Station.

50 Brimpton c.1900
This group of workers are removing bark from oak trees for use in the tanning industry. They have stopped in their work to pose with their special tools which include small axes, curved knives, and 'barking irons'. Stripping bark takes place when the sap is rising from late April until early June.

51 Brimpton c.1895 (right)
A local character, Frances Dyer, seen here cleaving branches for making hoops for wooden casks. Besides working as a general farm hand from March to October he also did woodland work during the winter months.

52

53

52 Lockinge c.1900
Before the introduction of machinery, hay making required a large number of workers in the fields. This group is haymaking on the Wantage Estate. The raking is done mainly by the women, whilst the men are involved with the cart loading and rickmaking in the background. The majority of the women are wearing the traditional country sun bonnet. This protected them from all extremes of weather, including sunburn which they considered most unbecoming.

53 Bucklebury c.1900
The name George W. Laily was famous throughout Berkshire and much of Britain well into the 20th century. His life and love was the traditional craft of the bowl turner, which had been handed down through his family. The products of his hands were not only for sale locally but could be purchased from such shops as Harrods. Many visitors came to Bucklebury particularly to see him at work.

54 Reading 1902
Huntley and Palmers Biscuit Factory. In one of the large biscuit cutting rooms, the mechanised conveyor belt system required concentration which it was unwise to break, even for a photograph. Up until 1918 the working week was 54 hours though this was not high in comparison with some factories. However I have already mentioned in my introduction the benefits enjoyed by the employees.

55 Twyford c.1903
The Fire Brigade are pictured outside their fire station on the corner of Wargrave Road, which was leased to them by Simonds the brewers. The captain Henry Maynard can be seen standing on the very left. Local records tell us that at this time the men were called together by a whistle although hoping eventually for a proper electric alarm bell. The steam fired engine itself had the intriguing name of the 'Stroller' and was drawn by two horses who were loaned to the brigade at a rate of two guineas a fire!

56 East Ilsley c.1906 (opposite)
The sheep fair. These fairs at East Ilsley date back to the reign of Henry III and became well-known throughout the country. The two largest fairs for sheep were held at Easter and Whitsun, and this photograph catches the dusty heat of the day. At its height up to 80,000 sheep were present at the fair, closely quartered in wooden pens, under the gaze of the shrewd buyer and the knowing shepherd. Many of the herds would have been walked great distances in order to be present.

57 East Ilsley c.1906
The sheep fair. The centre of interest focuses on the auctioneers' booth.
As can be seen the auctioneers, Waters and Rawlence, are not local but
have travelled up from Salisbury, highlighting the national importance of
these fairs. One of the outstanding features of this photograph is the
fashionable array of mens' hats – all characteristic of their period – the
straw boater, straw panama, the bowler, the cloth cap.

58 Berkshire 1905 (right)
This picture introduces not only the well-known figure of the postman,
but also another of the famous commercial names of the county – Sutton
Seeds. The photograph was actually taken to be used as an
advertisement, and the gentleman receiving the parcel of seeds is in fact
one of the Sutton family.

59 Barkham c.1907
The blacksmith, such as 'F East – shoeing and jobbing smith' here at Barkham, was a traditional sight in every village due to the dependence on horse power for travelling and agricultural work. The smithy was usually in a prominent position in the village so that it was easily accessible for custom both local and from the main road. Blacksmiths were well-informed characters due to the wide variety of people they met during their working day. The decline in horse traffic resulted in their need to take on more general repair work.

60 Yattendon 1910
The fire crew and their equipment pictured here, in comparison to Twyford (Photo 55), show the contrast in fire-fighting facilities available to villages of different sizes. Although taken at a later date, the smaller village of Yattendon still appears to have completely manual equipment. Unlike the brigades organised by the insurance companies whose clients paid for protection and received a special firemark denoting this to place on the front of their house, the village and parish brigades provided a voluntary service. It is recorded that during the 1870s more than one hundred voluntary fire brigades were formed in England and Wales

61   Uffington c.1910 (left)
The official school garden not far from St Mary's Church gave the opportunity for teaching, learning, and an additional supply of vegetables. Berkshire County Council obviously provided the gardening hut and wheelbarrow. The ratio of pupils to the area under cultivation seems rather high!

62   Theale 1915 (below)
A motor tractor at work on the land at Mill House Farm in these mid war years is a sign of the changing times. This type of tractor known as the Mogul was produced from 1912 to 1919. The model here was made by the American firm I.H.C. – International Harvester Corporation. The tractor plough behind, on the other hand, is a British product from Ransomes, the famous agricultural machinery firm of Ipswich, Suffolk.

63   Nr. Pusey c.1915
At this small brickworks the men are engaged in working a pug-mill and brickmaking machine, which was powered by the steam traction engine on the right. The products from large and small brickworks in Berkshire were in great demand with the increase in building of houses, schools, offices, and factories.

64   Twyford c.1916
During the 1st World War special sewing parties were organised to assist the war effort, as this one held outside the Assembly Rooms at Twyford.

People at Play

THE PACE of life was quickening throughout the Victorian period and by the turn of the century more time than ever before was being set aside for leisure pursuits. Those who benefited most noticeably were the new large social groups of people with independent incomes created by industrialisation and trade. For the bulk of the working classes opportunities for recreation were still very limited by lack of money and time, but changing ideas were gradually taking effect.

The introduction of the Bank Holiday in 1871 and the organised or work's outing by coach and carriage or by steamer on the Thames brought a new dimension to the word 'holiday'. The river offered many different opportunities for enjoyment. Rarely is there a photograph without some type of pleasure craft. Rowing regattas blossomed in popularity. Not only were there the major events as at Henley and Eton-and-Windsor but smaller clubs, such as the well organized working men's clubs, held their regattas at places all along the Thames including Streatley, Reading and Marlow.

The camera invariably catches the mood and atmosphere, the time of year and even the time of day, and of course the people themselves – whether participant or spectator – enjoying their time away from the routine of working hours.

65 Maidenhead c.1890
A holiday outing for the workers from the well-known firm of Stuchberrys, whose premises are in the background. The introduction of such holidays must have been greatly appreciated before the days of the official week's holiday with pay. It certainly appears that every male member of staff was attending as the charabanc carts could hardly seat more. The occasion was one for dressing in smart, if not best, clothing.

66 West Ilsley c.1890 (opposite top left)
Set against a traditional Berkshire landscape with the downs rising in the background, the children enjoy a moment of free time on a long summer's day. Two of the boys are wearing their elder sister's dresses following the custom of using handed-down clothing and can only be distinguished by their short hair and caps!

67 Streatley c.1895 (left)
The first of the famous Goring and Streatley regattas took place in August 1887. The occasion developed in the following years and frequently ended with a firework display.
This passage is from a prologue to a theatrical entertainment held at the 1892 regatta.

'Some are content to view this country fair,
And drink their fill of the most glorious air.
Others pull, punt and picnic on the stream,
And sail, and swim, and sun themselves and dream . . .
While here a masher with a shirt front pink
Sculling in high-starched collar makes me think
The days degenerate, compared with those
When men thought more of rowing than of clothes.
And now shall I describe that brilliant day
When to our challenge came a bright array
From London's clubs, from Moulsey's distant shore
From Henley's reach, famed for the bending oar
From Eton's classic strand, and keen to chance
The breathless struggle, and their fame enhance?'

68   Cold Ash c.1896 (previous page)
The Cold Ash hand-bell ringers may be taking part here in a local competition or purely adding to the merriment of a local fete. It was a hobby that different generations could pursue and enjoy together. The vicar (second from the left) would frequently be a member of the village team.

69   White Horse Hill c.1899 (below)
The traditional "scouring" of the White Horse and the festivities which accompanied it were held for the last time in 1857. However, a remnant of this tradition was maintained in the Bank Holiday fetes, for which many gathered on the hill from the surrounding villages in the Vale. The stalls here are catering for the pleasures of a holiday with their boxes of Fry's Chocolate and large tins of Huntley and Palmers biscuits. Quite why the man in the centre is wearing a woman's or possibly child's bonnet leads to intriguing speculation!

69

70

70   Abingdon c.1899
Skating on the river was a favourite pastime for men, women and children alike. Early photographs tend to show that the balance of the seasons was more extreme than it is today. The long and traditionally hot summer days gave way to more bitter winters with their frozen landscape. The problem of fitting and lacing skates was very satisfactorily overcome by bringing chairs onto the ice – which equally could be used for resting and for spectators. The chairs were also used for support; one skated along holding the back and pushing the chair in front.

71   Inkpen c.1900
   The brass band was an important element in village life. In smart uniform
   and well-equipped with instruments (often provided by the local gentry)
   it would be called upon to play at any special occasion. Young boys were
   frequently found as members of these bands. The number and variety in
   styles of moustaches in the photograph points clearly to another fashion
   of the day.

72   Maidenhead c.1900 (above right)
   Here, at the Cordwalles School physical exercises were performed to the
   accompaniment of music from the school band, standing in the shadow
   of the trees to the left of the photograph. The following passage is taken
   from a prospectus for the School:
   'The Rev. C R Carter . . . . assisted by an efficient
   staff of masters, receives into his house about 70 boys
   from the ages of 8 to 14½ to prepare for the Classical or
   Modern Sides of the Public Schools or for the Royal Navy.
   Boys have opportunities of learning Drawing, Carpentry,
   Gymnastics and Swimming, under properly qualified instructors.

73   Reading c.1900 (following page)
   The Museum, which opened to the public in 1883, in typical Victorian
   fashion used every available space to display its great variety of
   intriguing objects. An afternoon spent here could guarantee new
   discoveries each time, as it was impossible to take in all at one visit.

74 Streatley January 1st, 1902 (above)
The pastime of fox hunting has been firmly established in Berkshire since the mid 18th century.
The excitement for the spectator was brought to life in the following passage from 'A Peep at the Berkshire' by Castor. This appeared in the Sportsman February 1843, attributed to an Oxford undergraduate.
 'Just chancing this morning through Brightwell to stray
 I suddenly heard "Tally-Ho!" "Gone Away"
 When quickly in the body the Berkshire flew by,
 Their fox, just away, and "Forwards" the cry.
 Two hundred horsemen in the scene take a part,
 All cramming and nicking to get a good start.'

76 The Thames c.1912
A village outing from Shinfield by pleasure steamer on the Thames. There is a relaxed holiday atmosphere amongst the people here, young and old, friends and relatives, enjoying the summer's day out together. The bridge in the background is thought to be Wallingford.

75 Yattendon c.1910
At Burnt Hill Common, this non-conformist camp meeting was considered a day's outing for the family. Transport from the local villages included the wagonette on the left. Raised on the platform in the background are some of the day's speakers, including the Ashampstead postmaster and lay preacher, Mr Street, wearing a trilby hat.

People at Rest

A MIDST the bustle of life people found time to relax. The photographer's observing eye chose such moments, and often in these settings of peace and tranquillity he was able to crystalize a charactered face, particularly those of the elderly.

77

77   Bisham c.1890
The peace and quiet of the summer's day is captured with this small group of children. The older girls, though still children themselves were required to look after the younger members of the family. Aprons and pinafores were a practical fashion to keep clothes clean. Hats were worn possibly from choice but here more likely as a protection from the sun. Note the child's push-chair!

78

78   Moulsford c.1894
"There are few remains now of the old costumes characteristic of the Berkshire country, the fashions set by the numerous riverside visitors having a great influence on the dress of the inhabitants, but at Moulsford we saw several of the old style, and amongst them the long smock-frock, which was at the one time nearly universally worn by the Berkshire peasantry." H W Taunt "Goring, Streatley and the Neighbourhood". 1894

79   West Ilsley c.1895 (left)
The photographer has achieved a very good composition with the shape
of the doorway and the hedging framing the seated elderly figure.

80   West Ilsley c.1895 (above)
Dressed for the occasion, the oldest inhabitants of the village have been
persuaded to pose for their photograph. The Bath chair is a splendid
example of its kind.

81 Ashbury c.1901
The legend of Wayland's Smithy would have been better known than the fact that these stones were put together in prehistoric times to form a chambered tomb. The legend tells that horses could be left with a payment and on the owner's return would be found perfectly shod by the invisible craftsman, Wayland the Smith, who inhabited the 'cave'. The couple here have chosen a romantic setting for their meeting.

82 Reading July 1911
Whilst posing for this photograph during an outing to Prospect Park these proud grandparents were obviously unable to restrain their lively grandchild from moving.

The Berkshire Home: Cottage, Farm and Mansion

A HOME, however grand in stature or small in size, is always a direct link with the lives of past generations, the builder, and the subsequent inhabitants. Changes in architectural styles and building materials have become more noticeable over the last hundred years. Before this, traditions throughout the country continued unchallenged over the centuries. Once again the photograph played an important part in recording tradition and change. Traditional types of buildings and materials relate closely to particular areas. In parts of Berkshire for example, abundant and easily accessible resources of chalk and flint were frequently used with a 'hat' of thatch. Berkshire brick has been famous from its beginnings in the fourteenth century, but enjoyed a particular boost in output and popularity in the nineteenth century. Buildings of all types, from small cottages to large mansions, took advantage of this accommodating material.

Houses throughout history frequently have been altered and adapted to make them more useful for their present occupants. The crisp black and white early photographs can often highlight these changes. There are various reasons behind houses being totally demolished, whether from age and infestation, inconvenience from smallness or conversely from oversize. Many would have disappeared without any remaining evidence if it had not been for the ardent photographer. The fact that at times he was able to include the house-holders is an added bonus and pleasure.

83 Ashampstead c.1900
'The Row' is a traditional line of village cottages usually offering no more than 'two up, two down' accommodation. The number of children in the photograph causes us to remember the size of families brought up in such cottages.

84 Reading c.1904 (following page)
The town equivalent to the village cottage – the small terraced house – here in Western Road. These were built in their hundreds to cope with the demand for more housing following the great expansion of town population in the 19th century. There was a plentiful supply of local brick from the manufacturers in Reading which included S & E Collier at the Grovelands Kilns, and the Tilehurst Potteries at Kentwood Hill. Even on the smallest terrace there was frequently an area of special decorative brickwork – much favoured at this time – which can be seen here running beneath the upper floor windows.

85   Uffington c.1915 (above)
A family group taken outside their detached cottage. Built of local chalk
and brick, this was possibly thatched at one time. The use of slate as a
roofing material greatly increased in the second half of the 19th century
when the important source from North Wales was made accessible by the
railway.

86 Childrey c.1916
This type of cottage, here built of lath, plaster and brick, has its main accommodation on the ground floor. The small bedroom area under the steeply eaved thatched roof has limited light from the small windows at each end of the gable. The child can certainly be proud of his magnificent horse on wheels.

87 Shinfield c.1900
The interesting early Cut Bush farmhouse connects closely with the complex of working farm buildings. The construction of brick and timber under a tiled roof has an additional feature of a decorative porch at the front door.

88   Shellingford 1915
The farmhouse here has undergone a variety of alterations during its life.
A number of windows have been filled in, two different roofing materials
are at present in use – thatch and tile, and this photograph has caught a
moment during the rebuilding of the main chimney stack.

89   Winkfield c.1865 (above right)
Ascot Place was built in 1726 by Andrew Lindegen, a foreign wine
merchant from London. This area 'abounds with gentlemen's seats in
consequence of the beauty of the surroundings'. The popularity of this
part of Berkshire was also due to its accessibility to London. The
gentleman in the photograph is wearing a tall 'stove-pipe' hat, the
forerunner of the modern 'topper'.

90   Lockinge c.1898 (opposite)
A visit to Lockinge House by the Prince of Wales and Princess Alexandra
(standing in the centre on the first step). The house was the home of Lord
Wantage (standing fifth from the left) and Lady Wantage (who is just
behind the left shoulder of the Prince). The photographer has obviously
aimed at a casual rather that a stiffly posed photograph. The fashionable
dress of the day can be clearly seen, and it is interesting to note the veils
worn by many of the ladies with their high perched hats.

"Lockinge House is a very handsome mansion in mixed styles of
architecture built of red brick with stone dressing, standing in grounds of
167 acres which are tastefully laid out."
Kelly's Directory 1895

The Berkshire Home: Interiors

Although difficult to photograph, house interiors can give important details of the surroundings in which people lived.

Unfortunately the photographs here do not represent all types of interiors, for the cottage in particular was rarely taken. However these few show the typical Victorian attitude towards homely overfurnishing.

91   West Ilsley c.1895 (left)
The drawing room of West Ilsley House. This was decorated from floor to ceiling with heavily patterned wall-paper and mouldings. The ornamented mantelpiece and cast iron grate is surmounted by a vast mirror, a common feature of Victorian living rooms. Numerous small and large items of furniture offer an obstacle course about the room, and every available surface is covered with photographs and ornaments – memories of holidays and gifts from friends.

92   Shinfield c.1900 (above)
This photograph taken inside Shinfield Grange shows a typical Victorian evening scene. Reading aloud was popular, and many hours were spent in sewing and other handwork. The violin on the wall, and the piano reflect the enjoyment of family musical evenings.

The Berkshire Home: Gardens

A GARDEN to an Englishman has always been his own special domain. The Berkshire home-owner of yesterday was no exception. The following photographs and some preceding show the contrast between the large ornamental country mansion garden and the small highly functional cottage garden, where the vegetable plot was of prime importance.

93   Shinfield c.1900 (right)
The Grange. All country houses had large greenhouses which raised plants for their fine gardens. Here part of grape-vine is visible at the top of the picture.

"As the greenhouse would have given you a beautiful flower-garden and shrubbery during the winter, making the part of the house to which it is attached the pleasantest place in the world, so, in summer, what can be imagined more beautiful than bunches of grapes hanging down, surrounded by elegant leaves; and proceeding on each grapes from the size of a pin's head to the size of a plum". William Cobbett "The English Garden" 1829.

94   Shinfield c.1900 (following page)
The Grange. The lawn mower was introduced as an item of gardening equipment in the 1830s. The horse or donkey powered version was very necessary for large gardens with extensive areas of grass.

95   Reading c.1904 (left)
This town terrace house garden in Western Road, though small in size, is a mass of flowers and shrubs. These not only gave pleasure but also created a certain amount of privacy. Virginia creeper could be well employed to soften the otherwise harsh appearance of the brickwork. Photograph 84 shows this house from the front along with the owner and his dog.

96   Uffington c.1916 (above)
The main function of the cottage garden was the production of vegetables for the family. The gun held by the boy on the right may not be a toy, but rather for bird-scaring.

River and Canal

T HE waterways of Berkshire have always been a most important and visually attractive feature of its countryside. The natural rivers of the Thames and Kennet were supplemented with the canals – the Kennet and Avon, and the Wiltshire and Berkshire – to aid commercial transport.

The fascination of the river and its surroundings for the photographer has been mentioned already in connection with Henry Taunt. River life was a subject that offered scope to capture natural beauty, commercial traffic, and numerous pleasure pursuits. This made the Thames in particular one of the most photographed waterways in the country.

Locks, weirs, mills, and bridges held a romantic charm besides their functional use. The slow moving traditional barge and its horse or man power plodding along the towpath of river or canal conveys a feeling of unhurried time. Yet the commercial importance of these waterways for carrying all kinds of heavy goods, such as coal from the south west and Wales, must not be underestimated. It was the coming of the railways that began their gradual commercial decline. However in time a new user emerged – the pleasure boat. Photographs are a marvellous source of knowledge into the variety of small and large pleasure boats available. These were either made and sold by firms of boat builders along the river banks, or hired out for short trips from landing stages strategically placed at the most popular boating spots.

97 Caversham 1869
A view during the rebuilding of Caversham Bridge looking towards Caversham. The earlier bridge was described as 'the Oxford half an old fashioned stone and brick structure; the Berkshire half a sort of makeshift wood and iron skeleton'. Although one of the earliest photographs in this book, the detail in the foreground is extremely clear. It is one of a series taken to record the construction of the bridge.

98 Cookham c.1866
'Eel bucks' on the Hedsor flash lock. These were specially designed woven baskets for catching eels which were set up at various points along the river. These bucks belonged to Lord Boston, the landowner of this stretch of the Thames. The lady standing beside the small hut is wearing the style of full-skirted dress characteristic of the 1860's.

99 Hurley c.1875
The lock and lock-keeper's cottage. By the 1870s the need was recognized for special dwellings for lock-keepers adjacent to their work.

101   Pangbourne c.1890
The George Hotel landing stage on the Thames. The advertisement for the George Hotel in Henry Taunt's 'New Map of the River Thames' reads:-

'This House, being in the centre of the Picturesque Scenery of Pangbourne affords every accommodation for Tourists, Boating Parties or Anglers visiting the neightbourhood Wines and Spirits of the Finest Quality. Neat Flys and Broughams, Post Horses etc. James Bedding, Proprietor'.

100   Newbury c.1878
Newbury lock on the Kennet and Avon Canal, looking towards West Mills. The canal was built between 1794 and 1810 to assist good navigation along the Kennet and provide a very necessary link with the South West and Wales. It suffered with the coming of the Great Western Railway to Newbury in 1847 and shortly afterwards the canal company was forced to sell out to the railway.

102   Pangbourne c.1880 (previous page)
A traditional riverside scene with a horse-towed barge, which required very skilled steering from the barge itself. The photographer has even managed to pick up the detail of the actual tow-rope. In the background facing out across the river are the 'Seven Deadly Sins'. These are seven houses built in the 19th century which were criticised for spoiling an otherwise delightful stretch of the Thames. The argument for conservation is an old one.

103   Bray c.1885
The lock and weir being rebuilt in about 1885. Before it was remade the lock was described by Dickens as 'a rotten and dangerous structure'. The old flash-lock windlass still exists (in ruins) on the bank close above the weir.

104   Basildon c.1892
The jetty to Gatehampton. In the foreground the elderly man in the rowing boat may well be the official ferryman, C.Bossom, apparently called 'The Boss' by his friends. He worked the ferry from 1880 to 1894 when his son took over the post. The ferry boat itself is tied up on the opposite bank and nearby is the neat small ferry-house which was rebuilt in 1891 just before this photograph was taken.

106   Old Windsor c.1893
An electric launch charging station situated in The Thames off Magna Carta Island. The firm of Immish Launch & Boat Company Ltd. was founded in 1887. Their headquarters was at Hampton-on-Thames and they were the first company to introduce electrically propelled launches. To overcome the difficulty of recharging boat batteries, they equipped several floating charging stations such as this which could be moored at various points along the river.

105   Bray c.1890
Edward Morris, Lock-keeper from 1881 to 1894. This photograph epitomises the strength and natural good humour which is often associated with the lock-keepers along the Thames. The homemade lemonade and ginger beer would have been a profitable side-line, particularly with the customers from the pleasure boats.

107   Streatley c.1890 (following page)
In the late 19th century watermills were still a frequent sight along the Thames. The miller at Streatley at this time was Charles Hobbs. Characteristic of the Thames mills, the barge here is unloading on the upstream side. Before it burnt down in 1926, Streatley mill was a popular subject for the artist and the photographer.

108   Maidenhead c.1893
   It is said that by the late 1880s there were about 250 steam pleasure
launches travelling up and down the Thames. Although these provided a
convenient method of travelling for many, they were very disliked by
other river users. Dickens espresses here the feelings of the day:-
        'Steam launches are too often the curse of the river. Driving
        along at an excessive rate of speed, with an utter disregard for
        the comfort of and necessities of anglers, oarsmen, and boating
        parties, the average steam launch engineer is an unmitigated
        nuisance.'

109   Maidenhead c.1910
   Boat builders and hiring stages were a well-known sight along the
Thames, and commercial advertisements for these often appear in the
early books on the river and local directories. Henry Wilder and Son
started this business shortly before the turn of the century.

110 Wantage c.1895
The Wilts and Berks Canal in Mill Street. This canal not only served the
adjacent country areas, but acted as an important link to the South West,
to the potteries via the North Wilts Canal. Seen here is a large commercial
barge belonging to the Wantage Coal Merchant William Hiskins. The
collection of chimney pots and bricks on the quayside are likely to be
products of a local brickworks awaiting transportation.

Road

THE condition of the roads in nineteenth century Berkshire was varied. The principal routes to London, Oxford, Newbury, and of course Bath, taking coach, carriage and some wagon traffic, were usually kept in good repair. Some of the smaller roads, particularly in the east of the county, are also known to have been well maintained. However, the country roads towards the west and in the Vale of the White Horse were narrower. Picturesque to the artist and the photographer in the summer, they became deeply rutted and impassable in the winter months. The sometimes romantic views in photographs therefore should be seen in this context.

In the early years of photography the horse was still the main means of power for carriage, coach, and cart. One is often made aware of the close relationship between the driver and his steed. The end of the century saw changes to 'horse-power' of a different kind. Steam was the new form of road transport, particularly for heavy goods, but this in its turn was superseded by the motor vehicle in its many private and commercial guises.

A special mention must be made of the variety of cycles noticeable in many early photographs. These varied from the solid delivery types – often a tricycle with a basket or carrier's box – to the ordinary pleasure cycle for one or two. Apart from the leisure aspects of the cycle clubs, the bicycle gave the poorer elements of society greater mobility than ever before. They were able to look wider for work and leisure without moving their homes. In the early days many villages had firms which hired bicycles.

111   Streatley c.1885
This photograph of the coachman Pratt, and his horse and carriage, was taken outside Streatley House, which at the time belonged to the Morrell family. Houses of this size would have had at least one coachman and carriage.

112 Wittenham Clumps c.1890 (opposite)
A truly rural roadside view with Wittenham Clumps receding into a misty background. Here the photographer has caught the central activity of the elderly walking couple, and the horse drawn plough with its team of man and boy. The road leading to the village is in comparatively good condition, although it still has an unmetalled surface.

113 Maidenhead c.1895 (below left)
Situated at the station end of King Street, the cab rank of carriages is suitably placed for customers arriving by train. The four seater Hackney carriage, hired with a driver, was a popular form of transport in towns throughout the country. The building in the background 'Lookers Dining and Refreshment Rooms' provided another important facility for travellers.

114 Reading c.1900
This substantial steam powered lorry was used by the Reading Mill owners Soundy and Son for their delivery work. In about 1890 the cost of traction engine haulage was ld to 3d per ton per mile, which was cheaper than horse haulage by about 50 per cent. The decline in the use of steam transport was due to a number of reasons. These included an increase in taxes on vehicles by weight, the time taken to raise steam, the necessity of a two man crew, and the tendency for boiler accidents; all of which put them at an increasing disadvantage with the developing motor vehicles.

113

114

115

115   East Ilsley c.1895 (opposite)
Looking across the downs with East Ilsley windmill standing out on the skyline. This beautiful sweeping view of the Berkshire countryside acclaims the artistic merits of the early photographer, in this case Henry Taunt. At this time the miller was Frederick Prior, but by 1907 the mill had been left to fall into disrepair.

116   Maidenhead c.1895 (above left)
Timberlakes Cycleworks in Queen Street. The original firm was started by Thomas T. Timberlake in 1867, and continued until 1962. Nos. 85 and 87 Queen Street were built by the family as workshops where they produced bicycles and tricycles such as those pictured here. This photograph was taken a few years after the Timberlake brothers famous "long ride" in 1890 from Queen Street to Edinburgh, each carrying 20 lbs, of luggage. The small shop next door belonging to De La Hay advertises her as 'Ladies Habits and Breeches Maker'.

117   Reading c.1900 (above)
A Huntley and Palmers carrier van drawn up outside the factory in Reading. In the early days Huntley and Palmers contracted their delivery work to Pickfords before introducing their own special vans. These had the traditional tarred canvas 'tilt' with small circular glass windows in the sides. The similarly designed railway carriers vans were a frequent sight in towns, where they bridged the gap between the railhead and the customer.

118

119

118   Twyford c.1920
This smart motor delivery van belonged to the Twyford baker and grocer
J Webb and Co. It highlights the changeover from the delivery horse and
cart to the modern motor vehicle. The employee on the left carries a
traditional delivery basket.

119   Twyford 1910
The driver of this millers' wagon and his small helper have stopped for
refreshments at Warren House crossroad between Twyford and Binfield.
Lawrence Davis Ltd. was a well established milling business based at
Twyford Mill.

Rail

BERKSHIRE's railway system was dominated by the Great Western Railway. Despite early opposition, particularly from the Thames commissioners, canal and coach proprietors, and certain towns who could see no personal benefit, the plans to link Bristol with London, drawn up by Isambard Kingdom Brunel, were set in motion. In 1838 Maidenhead station was opened, linking the county to the capital. Two years later saw the completion of the line to Reading with the personal attention of Brunel and a party of directors on the trial run. Further important extensions were provided during that decade by the opening of Didcot Junction and the line through the Kennet Valley to Newbury and Hungerford. All opposition to the new means of transport soon collapsed as people appreciated the immense benefits that it brought in its wake. By the end of the century there were hardly any towns or villages in Berkshire that did not have easy access to a railway station, from which one could travel quickly to most parts of the country.

The camera and the railway were children of the same era, and developing together could complement one another's achievements. The early stations, single track lines and locomotives, with the attendant railway staff and excited passengers, offered the photographer new and challenging subjects. The scene often required as wide an angled view as possible to do justice to the detail. The familiar problem of movement frequently occurs in railway photographs, not to mention the hazard of a sudden spurt of steam or billow of smoke.

120   Windsor c.1885

These goods carriages are on the Windsor branch of the South Western Railway which had its terminus immediately at the base of the castle. It is recorded as having a private entrance made from the grounds "for the convenience of Her Majesty".

121

122

121   Lambourn c.1900
The Lambourn Valley Railway was opened in 1898 as an independent line connecting with the Great Western Railway at Newbury. This photograph of the station and railway staff was taken before the G.W.R. acquired the line in 1905 after which new buildings were constructed. The passenger train service was finally withdrawn in 1960, but part of the line remained open for goods traffic until 1965. The railside advertisements tell us that Sutton seeds were distributed by post and rail direct from Sutton and Sons, Reading, without the use of agents.

122   Reading c.1902
To assist the transporting of their biscuits and other necessary goods such as fuel, Huntley and Palmers constructed a small branch railway from their factory to the railhead at Reading's mainline station. As can be seen here, they had special engines and goods trucks marked with the firm's name.

123   Didcot c.1904 (opposite)
The famous junction on the Great Western Railway branching here from London to the North and West. This was opened on June 12th 1844.

124

125

124 Uffington c.1914
The station at Uffington was an important stopping point for the Vale of the White Horse on the Great Western Railway between Didcot and Swindon. From here there was a branch line up to Faringdon. Awaiting collection on the platform are a number of the large 17 gallon milk churns. Milk was an essential shipment from the country to the town which was made possible for the first time by the railway. Prior to the railway, fresh milk in the larger towns was supplied by town dairies using stall fed cows. There was a marked effect on the rural economy since the milk cheque brought a regular cash income to the dairying areas at a time when increasing imports of cheap agricultural products were helping to cause a major depression in the farming world.

125 East Garston c.1920
A typical country station on the outskirts of the village, with only a small waiting shelter and nearby level crossing. This was situated on the Lambourn Valley line between Great Shefford and Eastbury Halt.

126 Wokingham c.1905 (opposite)
There is an excited stir amongst the passengers on the platform as the train draws into the station. In 1903 the Staines and Woking railway, joining the South Western line at Staines, gave access to London from Wokingham in 1½ hours.

126

Celebrations

OR THE Victorian photographer these occasions were indeed a challenge. The subjects were frequently unique, but the possibility of movement, whether animal, human, or merely a flag caught in a gust of wind, was inevitable. The success and clarity of these photographs is, therefore, something to be highly commended. The atmosphere of the occasion comes out to us, and draws us back into the photograph. The excited gaiety of the people is definitely infectious. The costume is always worthy of a closer look. 'Sunday best' was naturally worn on these occasions. Everyday clothes were of necessity functional and frequently 'the worst for wear', so the enjoyment of being 'well dressed' and 'in fashion' was very real and is well conveyed in these pictures.

127 Uffington 1st May 1916
The traditions of May Day celebrations were strongly maintained in Berkshire, having managed to survive opposition during the Puritan rule. Uffington was one of the last villages to have a genuine early Maypole in the nineteenth century. This was temporarily stolen by the neighbouring village of Ashbury. Unfortunately its reinstatement was short lived as the vicar of the time felt that it was more necessary for the pole to be cut up and given to the poor women of the parish for fuel! Fortunately here the village children have revived the custom.

128

128   Abingdon 1887 (previous page)
To celebrate the 1887 Jubilee a less imposing obelisk in the town square was replaced by this statue of Queen Victoria – a day worthy of immortalizing in a photograph. The moment caught shows the statue yet to be unveiled, the crowd awaiting the words from the dais in the centre. The town band can be seen to the left of the statue.

129   Shinfield 1887
The Daffodil Party at Shinfield Grange is an example of private festivity which grew into an annual event. On a spring day each year the owners of the Grange invited their family and friends to meet and gather armfuls of wild daffodils in Hidend Road Copse.

130   Reading c.1890
A circus parade causes great excitement as it moves along Broad Street. The circus had developed in popularity from the end of the eighteenth century. The introduction of wild animals gave a separate attraction of a menagerie to which the public were admitted for an extra charge. Performing animals became common after the 1840s.

131   Maidenhead 1897
Many towns responded to the Diamond Jubilee celebrations with natural enthusiasm, which included decorating the streets with large flags and other bunting. Here in the High Street the photographer has set his camera to record the festive decorations and attracted a small crowd, mainly of children, eager to appear in the photograph. It is fortunate that yet another photographer took this complete scene.

132 Wallingford 1897
Street parties were a popular Jubilee celebration. The one shown in this photograph was held in the Market Place.

133 Maidenhead 1897 (above right)
To celebrate Queen Victoria's Jubilee, Keyes Brewery produced their own decoration in the form of this magnificent arch made from beer barrels of varying sizes.

134 Wantage 1898 (opposite)
From a high vantage point the photographer has managed to encompass a wide view of this visit to the town by Edward Prince of Wales and Princess Alexandra. The couple are seated in the carriage to the right of the centre, which has stopped to allow the presentation of a bouquet of flowers. The children raised on a platform around the Alfred Statue sang the National Anthem when the royal couple arrived. The music was supplied by the band tightly packed into the large cart behind the statue!

THE OLD POST OFFICE VAULTS
ALLSOPPS FINE ALES AND STOUT
FREE HOUSE JOSEPH THEURAN
WINES AND PORTS

135

135 Thatcham 1902
In celebration of the Coronation of King Edward VII in August 1902 festivities, including this seated open-air meal, were held in the Broadway and on the Green.

Acknowledgements

Photographic sources: The Author and the Publisher wish to thank the following individuals and organisations for allowing copies to be made of original photographs in their possession or for supplying prints:

Mrs J Ball, 118
Berkshire Archaeological Society, 9, 14, 15, 19, 21, 28, 31, 32, 35, 36, 37, 40, 41, 42, 49, 56, 57, 63, 66, 69, 70, 74, 77, 79, 80, 81, 86, 88, 91, 101, 107, 110, 112, 115, 123, 125, 128, 134
Miss E Brooks, 64
Miss Carter, 71
Mrs Doe, 83
Mr T Goodwin, 119
Mr P Horsburgh, 25
Huntley and Palmers, 54, 117, 122
Lacock Abbey Collection (Fox Talbot Museum of Photography), 1
Mrs Leech, 38
Maidenhead Reference Library, 65
Museum of English Rural Life, 46, 50, 51, 52, 53, 58, 62
Mrs Mott, 60
National Monuments Record, 89
Newbury District Museum, 39
Oxford City Library, 10, 12, 26, 29, 43, 44, 45, 61, 67, 72, 78, 85, 96, 99, 100, 102, 103, 104, 105, 106, 111, 120, 124, 127
Mr B Parsons, 68, 135
Mr J Penfold, 18, 121
Reading Museum and Art Gallery, 2, 3, 4, 5, 6, 7, 17, 20, 23, 24, 34, 73, 97, 126
Reading Reference Library (Berkshire Local History Collection), 22, 33, 59, 90, 114, 130
Mr J S Spink, 8, 76, 87, 92, 93, 94, 129
Mr W G Stewart, 16
Thames Water (Thames Conservancy Division), 98
Twyford and Ruscombe Local History Society, 55
Mr M Underhill, 11, 13, 27, 30, 47, 48, 108, 109, 113, 116, 131, 132, 133
Collection of the late Mr R Wyatt with the permission of Mrs Wyatt, 75
Author, 82, 84, 95

The Author wishes to record her thanks to the following for their valuable assistance and kindness in the preparation of this book:

Mr J Creasey (M.E.R.L.)
Mrs P Curtis (Maidenhead Reference Library)
Mr J Finch (Twyford and Ruscombe Local History Society)
Mr F M Gilbertson
Mr M Graham (Oxford City Library)
Mr and Mrs R Greenaway
Mr M Hall (Thames Water)
Mr A Higgott (Newbury District Museum)
Mrs V Howse
Mrs J Hunter (Berkshire Local History Association)
Mr R Lassam (Fox Talbot Museum)
Mr I Leith (National Monuments Record)
Mr J K Major
Mr B Parsons
Mr M Paxton (Huntley and Palmers)
Mr J Penfold
Miss D Phillips (Reading Reference Library)
Mrs A Railton
Mrs C Reeve (Maidenhead Archaeological & Historical Society)
Mr J S Spink
Mr W G Stewart
Dr S Ward (M.E.R.L.)
Mr M Underhill

Berkshire Federation of Women's Institutes

The Author would like to acknowledge the great help and encouragement received from her colleagues at Reading Museum and Art Gallery. She is particularly grateful to Mr C Sizer, Mr C L Cram and Mr M Andrews, and to Mrs B Mair and Mrs D Baker for their patience in typing the script.

She is also extremely indebted to the publishers, Nicholas and Suzanne Battle.

Index of Places
by page number

Abingdon, 21, 52, 89
Aldworth, 29
Ashampstead, 59
Ashbury, 58

Barkham, 47
Basildon, 72
Bisham, 29, 56
Bradfield, 35
Bray, 30, 72, 73
Brimpton, 42
Bucklebury, 43

Caversham, 68
Charney Bassett, 37
Childrey, 38, 61
Cold Ash, 51
Cookham, 28, 69

Didcot, 85

East Garston, 86
East Ilsley, 34, 45, 46, 80
East Hagbourne, 33

Faringdon, 16

Goosey, 32

Hinton Waldrist, 38
Hungerford, 12, 22
Hurley, 69

Inkpen, 53

Lambourn, 84
Lockinge, 43, 63

Maidenhead, 18, 19, 40,
    50, 53, 75, 79, 81, 91, 92
Moulsford, 56

Newbury, 19, 20, 41, 70
North Hinksey, 28

Old Windsor, 73

Pangbourne, 32, 70, 71
Pusey, 49

Reading, 9, 11, 12, 13, 22,
    24, 25, 40, 44, 54, 58, 60,
    67, 79, 81, 84, 90

Ruscombe, 27

Shellingford, 62

Shinfield, 13, 61, 64, 65,
    66, 90
Shrivenham, 35
Stanford-in-the-Vale, 36
Sonning, 31
Steventon, 26
Streatley, 51, 54, 74, 77

Thatcham, 94
Theale, 48
Three Mile Cross, 31
Twyford, 44, 49, 82

Uffington, 48, 60, 67,
    86, 88

Wallingford, 24, 55, 92
Waltham St Lawrence, 30
Wantage, 23, 76, 93
West Ilsley, 51, 57, 64
White Horse Hill, 52
Windsor, 10, 18, 83
Winkfield, 62
Wittenham, 39
Wittenham Clumps, 78
Wokingham, 21, 87

Yattendon, 34, 47, 55